# Blending Career into Relationship

Maintaining Strong Bond in a Relationship Despite the Burden Your Career

Throws at You

Adegboye S. Aduragbemi

# INTRODUCTION

In the modern world, many couples attempt, with varied degrees of success, to walk the fine line between the responsibilities of family life and the demands of a career. Amidst the everyday chaos of life, balancing professional goals, meetings, deadlines, and quality time with loved ones can pose challenges to communication, prioritization, and harmony maintenance. "Career and Work-Life Balance FAQ in Marriage" guides married couples who are trying to figure out how to balance their obligations to each other and their careers. It offers clarity, understanding, and valuable advice.

This book contains a thorough list of frequently asked questions, thoughtful responses, and professional guidance specific to the complexities of striking a balance between work and family life in the context of marriage. Each question is answered with compassion, comprehension, and practical advice to assist couples in managing the intricacies of career and work-life balance with grace and intentionality. Topics range from managing stress and burnout to coordinating career objectives with shared values.

"Career and Work-Life Balance FAQ in Marriage" gives married couples a road map for promoting mutual support, keeping lines of communication open, and putting their relationship first despite the pressures of work life through relevant tales, real-world experiences, and evidence-based tactics. Whether you're pursuing an entrepreneurial endeavour, managing a dual-career home, or moving up the corporate ladder, this book offers priceless insights and valuable tools to help you negotiate the challenges of work-life balance and career with perseverance, confidence, and love.

May you find comfort in the experiences of others who have gone before you, inspiration in the knowledge of professionals, and the bravery to accept professional achievement and marital fulfilment as complimentary cornerstones of a happy life together as you set out on this path of research and discovery. Together, let's explore the ageless issues, complex dynamics, and beauty of striking a balance between a married couple's obligations to one another and their careers.

# Chapter One

## Balancing your career and home

*Building your relationship on a solid foundation*

Sarah and Alex were two people in the busy metropolis of Metroville whose career paths unexpectedly crossed, resulting in a partnership based on aspiration, respect for one another, and a shared dedication to work-life harmony. They first connected at a business networking event where Alex, a committed software engineer aiming for success, and Sarah, a motivated marketing executive with a passion for her work, were drawn to each other's aspirations and ambitions.

During their early exchanges, they were highly intellectually stimulating and supportive of each other's achievements. Sarah was impressed by Alex's creative thinking and his commitment to his profession. At the same time, Alex was enthralled with Sarah's leadership qualities and her poise and confidence in navigating the corporate world.

With increasing time spent together, Sarah and Alex came to realize how crucial work-life balance is to success and happiness. They became close via their shared struggles to balance challenging occupations with personal fulfilment, and they took comfort in the encouragement and support of one another.

As they overcame the difficulties of striking a balance between their personal and professional goals, their relationship grew. Despite their hectic schedules, Sarah and Alex deliberately found time for each other, setting aside times of leisure and relaxation. They encouraged one another's professional ambitions since they understood that their happiness as a pair depended on their ability to succeed professionally.

As their love grew, Sarah and Alex committed themselves to one another by exchanging vows in front of loved ones in a touching ceremony. They accepted their positions as partners in life and their careers, knowing that their love and mutual knowledge of each other's goals would help them overcome any difficulties that may arise.

Years later, Sarah and Alex proudly and gratefully reflected on their experience. They were aware that their mutual respect, understanding, and dedication to work-life balance had served as the cornerstones of their partnership. With their love and support for one another, they believed they could overcome any challenge and realize their aspirations together. Their bond had only gotten stronger over time.

This summary highlights the value of mutual support, understanding, and communication in creating a solid and long-lasting connection by showing how a relationship may be built on a foundation of shared career objectives and a dedication to work-life balance.

## Career goal competition: the enemy of a successful relationship

Sarah and James were once considered the perfect power couple in the vibrant metropolis of Metroville. After meeting in graduate school, they fell madly in love and decided to take on the world as a couple. But as they went after their separate careers, competing goals and agendas caused their partnership to fall apart.

Driven and passionate about justice, Sarah put a lot of effort into her employment, putting in long hours on the weekends and late nights to advance in the company. James was a gifted architect who dreamed of opening his own business. He gave his everything to his work and neglected their relationship to pursue his career aspirations.

Their different job goals seemed like a slight annoyance at first, but as they experienced disappointments and celebrated victories, tensions grew. They were always at odds over money matters, priorities in their lives, and the trade-offs they were ready to make for their professions. Their once-loving relationship turned into a never-ending loop of discontent, hatred, and finger-pointing.

One fateful evening, their dispute over moving to accept James's job offer turned into a full-fledged showdown, bringing their career-related difficulties to a peak. Feeling conflicted about her commitment to her job and her marriage, Sarah became irate and accused James of putting his goals ahead of their union. James, who felt misinterpreted and unsupported, retaliated angrily, demanding that Sarah put their relationship ahead of her professional goals.

As the years went by, there was no longer any sign of love or connection between Sarah and James as their relationship continued to worsen due to their arguments. They made a valiant effort to save their marriage, but it was in vain. They tried career counselling, couples therapy, and even a trial separation. Ultimately, they both lamented the loss of the love they had previously experienced when they made the painful decision to separate ways.

Years later, Sarah and James coincidentally crossed paths once more. They couldn't help but feel a twinge of grief for the love they had lost as they made small talk. They acknowledged that their failure to strike a balance between their devotion to one another and their professional goals had ruined their relationship, and they regretted not having placed a higher priority on open communication, flexibility, and support for one another early on.

This summary shows how competing career goals may strain even the strongest of bonds, emphasizing the value of open communication and willingness to make concessions and support one another in building a solid and long-lasting alliance.

# Chapter Two

*Prioritizing a career above your home*

**How can we prioritize our relationships and family lives over the demands of our careers?**

Prioritization, time management, and good communication are crucial to juggling the demands of both work and family life. Talk plainly with your partner about your goals for your profession and your objectives as a family. Work together to make a schedule that makes time for quality time spent together. Create limits between your personal and professional lives, and give priority to the things that strengthen your family ties and relationships.

**How can we keep our relationship balanced and encourage each other's professional aspirations?**

Empathy, support, and adaptability are necessary to help each other advance in our jobs. Show interest in your partner's professional goals and, if required, provide both practical and emotional support. Openly discuss your wants and job

11

objectives with your partner, then work together to come up with solutions that prioritize your partnership while satisfying the desires of both of you.

**How do we approach circumstances in which our family life is negatively impacted by one partner's work requiring more time or travel?**

Cooperation, communication, and compromise are necessary to manage disparities in career demands. Recognize how one partner's work obligations affect the family and talk about how to balance spending time apart with staying in touch. When you have time to spend together, please make the most of it by prioritizing quality time and being flexible with schedules and commitments.

**How can we keep stress at work from harming our relationships and overall health?**

Maintaining open communication, establishing boundaries, and engaging in self-care are all necessary to prevent stress at work. Make time for things that make you happy and fulfilled outside of work, and give priority to self-care activities that assist you in unwinding and recharging. Share your wants and stressors with your partner honestly and openly, then work together to discover solutions that will enhance each other's well-being.

**What supportive atmosphere can we provide to foster our relationship and help both partners succeed in their careers?**

Respect for one another, encouragement, and common objectives are necessary to establish a helpful atmosphere. Honour one another's successes and life events, and provide assistance and inspiration when things go tough. Make it a priority to have open conversations about needs and job objectives. Work together to develop a schedule and atmosphere that lets both partners achieve their goals and make time for each other a priority.

**How do we handle disputes resulting from different expectations or priorities for one's profession, such as when one partner wants more outstanding work-life balance while the other wants to develop their career?**

Effective communication, understanding, and compromise are necessary for conflict management. Find common ground by first candidly discussing each partner's expectations and professional aspirations. Examine alternative agreements that preserve a positive work-life balance while enabling both couples to feel encouraged in their professional ambitions. Recognize and respect one another's viewpoints by modifying expectations.

**How can we make sure that the choices we make about our careers complement our long-term objectives and our family and relationship vision?**

Regular introspection, goal setting, and candid communication are necessary to ensure alignment. Make time to talk about your long-term objectives, both personal and professional, both individually and together. Try to make decisions about your job that are in line with your shared future vision, taking into account the effects that it may have on your relationships and family dynamics. To maintain continuous harmony and alignment, be prepared to review and modify your objectives as necessary.

**How can we prioritize our relationships and personal welfare without sacrificing our feelings of balance and joy in our careers?**

Setting boundaries, being self-aware, and purposefully prioritizing tasks are all necessary to maintain balance. Evaluate your commitments and job decisions on a regular basis to see how they affect your general well-being and relationship happiness. Establish limits on expectations from the workplace and give self-care activities that support fulfilment and balance a priority. Openly discuss your needs and goals with your spouse, and work together to establish a nurturing environment that supports each other's success on both a personal and professional level.

**How can we take care of our relationship as a couple and also feel like we are individuals with fulfilment in our careers?**

In retaining your unique personality, there is a need for self-awareness, setting limits, and making a conscious effort to invest in your relationship. Give top priority to extracurricular pursuits and interests that advance personal development and fulfilment. Openly discuss your needs and goals with your partner, and work together to establish a nurturing environment that lets each partner follow their hobbies while also making time for quality time spent together. To strengthen a feeling of encouragement and support among one another, don't forget to acknowledge and celebrate each other's successes, both personally and professionally.

**What should we do when one partner's success or career growth surpasses the other's, causing feelings of uneasiness or envy?**

Managing feelings of jealousy or insecurity calls for cooperation in goalsetting, empathy, and assurance. Start by accepting and confirming one another's emotions and experiences without passing judgment. Establish open lines of communication regarding your goals and concerns, then work together to develop a strategy for fostering each other's professional development. Instead of measuring yourself against your partner or feeling intimidated by their accomplishments, concentrate on appreciating each other's victories and achievements. Recall that shared development, encouragement, and support are more important indicators of a successful relationship than individual accomplishments.

**Rather than concentrating only on monetary gain or social expectations, how can we make sure that our job decisions are in line with our values and priorities as a couple?**

Regular introspection, goal setting, and deliberate decision-making are necessary to ensure alignment. Set aside some time to talk about your priorities and values as a pair with regard to your personal and professional lives. Think about how your professional decisions affect your family objectives, overall well-being, and your relationship dynamics. Make an effort to make choices that are consistent with your shared goals and values rather than relying only on outside influences like money or social pressures. If necessary, review and modify your career objectives to maintain continuous alignment and satisfaction as a partnership.

**How can we help each other's professional development by utilizing our different networks, experiences, and skill sets from our careers?**

Working together, communicating, and supporting one another is necessary to utilize each other's strengths fully. Show that you are interested in your partner's professional ambitions and aspirations by showing support and encouragement when required. Give your partner access to ideas, contacts, and experiences that could help them grow in their job. Work together on initiatives or projects that make the most of each partner's knowledge and expertise. As a team, remember to acknowledge and be grateful for each other's contributions and to enjoy each other's accomplishments.

**How can we generate a warm and inclusive workplace that honours and promotes the talents and professional goals of both partners?**

Advocacy, dialogue, and respect for one another are all necessary to cultivate a helpful work environment. Show a keen interest in one another's work experiences and difficulties, and extend assistance and motivation as required. Encourage your employer to implement inclusive strategies and procedures that take into explanation the needs and viewpoints of all employees. Work together on activities or projects that showcase the skills and abilities of both parties. To foster a spirit of gratitude and support among one another, don't forget to acknowledge and celebrate each other's successes in both your personal and professional lives.

**With the rigours and responsibilities of our different occupations, how can we keep our relationship feeling intimate and connected?**

Consciously making an effort, talking, and spending quality time together are necessary to maintain connection. Make it a priority to check in frequently to talk about how each spouse is feeling and what they need to feel appreciated and supported. Whether it's a romantic evening, a weekend escape, or just spending time together at home, set aside specific time for intimate and connecting experiences. In order to prioritize your relationship and maintain your connection despite the demands of your careers, be prepared to modify your schedules and obligations as necessary; recall that investing in your partnership is essential for your long-term contentment and happiness together.

**When faced with demands or expectations from outside sources, how can we make sure that our professional decisions are in line with our values and priorities as a couple?**

Sharing decisions, communicating, and reflecting are all necessary to ensure alignment. Talk about your priorities and guiding principles as a pair, including your personal and professional lives. Think about how your professional decisions affect your family objectives, overall well-being, and your relationship dynamics. Be prepared to deviate from social norms in order to make choices that are consistent with your shared goals and beliefs. Have faith in your collaboration and place a high value on honest communication to overcome any obstacles or doubts that may surface.

**Especially during hectic or stressful times, how can we keep our relationship feeling intimate and connected despite the rigours and strains of our different careers?**

Consciously making an effort, talking, and spending quality time together are necessary to maintain connection. Make it a priority to check in frequently to talk about how each spouse is feeling and what they need to feel appreciated and supported. Whether it's a romantic evening, a weekend escape, or just spending time together at home, set aside specific time for intimate and connecting experiences. In order to prioritize your relationship and maintain your connection despite the demands of your careers, be prepared to modify your schedules and obligations as necessary. Recall that investing in your partnership is essential for your long-term contentment and happiness together.

# Chapter Three

*Effectively handling transition moments without jeopardizing your home*

**As a couple, how do we handle career transitions or changes like job loss?**

Resilience, flexibility, and teamwork are necessary for navigating professional shifts. See transitions as chances for development and fresh starts, and rely on one another for both practical and emotional support. Talk candidly about your hopes and worries, and work together to develop a strategy for getting through the change.

**How can we make sure that neither partner feels ignored or unsatisfied and that our personal and professional lives are balanced?**

Maintaining equilibrium calls for consistent check-ins, reciprocal assistance, and shared goals. Plan frequent check-ins to find out how each spouse is feeling about the work-life balance, and be prepared to modify commitments and schedules as necessary. Make time for each other and activities that deepen your relationship a priority. Encourage one another to pursue interests and hobbies outside of work.

**How do we manage circumstances where one spouse has to give up something or compromise in other parts of our relationship or personal lives in order to progress or succeed in their career?**

Negotiation, empathy, and common goalsetting are necessary for handling concessions or sacrifices. Start by expressing and affirming each other's emotions and worries around the potential effects on your relationship and the personal health of one spouse advancing in their job. Talk honestly about how you can encourage one another's ambitions while still finding fulfilment and balance in other facets of your lives. To meet the needs and goals of both partners, be prepared to compromise and reorder priorities as necessary. Prioritize mutual support, harmony, and your partnership's growth when coming up with solutions.

**How do we resolve disputes or conflicts about priority or career decisions?**

Empathy, active listening, and compromise are necessary for handling conflicts. Approach arguments with an open mind, be willing to hear the other person out and be honest about your demands and concerns. To keep your relationship harmonious, look for areas of agreement and cooperative solutions that respect each partner's goals and values. It would be best if you also were prepared to make concessions and change your expectations when necessary.

**How can we encourage each other's professional development and objectives without becoming threatened or competing with one another's achievements?**

Mutual trust, encouragement, and a feeling of shared cooperation are necessary for mutual support. Start by being honest with each other about your unique career aims and goals, as well as how you can help each other to achieve them. Honour one another's accomplishments and anniversaries and provide support and encouragement as required. Encourage

25

cooperation rather than rivalry and acknowledge that the achievements of both partners influence the relationship's general well-being and happiness. Keep in mind that you are a team and that your successes are a result of your mutual support and dedication to one another.

**In order to handle unforeseen obstacles or changes in our relationships and employment, how can we develop resilience and adaptability?**

Maintaining constant communication, adaptability, and a growth mentality are necessary for building resilience. View obstacles or changes as chances for personal development and education for both you and your partner. Make it a priority to have candid conversations about navigating uncertainty and setbacks together and work together to develop a plan for handling problems as they come up. Remind each other to support and encourage one another and acknowledge your joint accomplishment of overcoming challenges.

**When one or both partners are under a lot of strain at work, how do we handle the effects of career-related stress on our relationship?**

Coping mechanisms, communication, and empathy are all essential components of stress management. Commence by recognizing and validating one another's experiences and feelings around stress at work. Establish a nurturing atmosphere where both partners are at ease communicating their feelings and asking for help when they need it. Together, determine which stress reduction strategies work best, such as exercising, practising mindfulness, or consulting a therapist or counsellor. To offset the negative impacts of stress on your relationship, give priority to spending quality time together and engaging in activities that foster connection and relaxation.

**Rather than concentrating just on outward metrics of success or achievement, how can we make sure that our job decisions enhance our total wellness and satisfaction as a couple?**

Self-evaluation, dialogue, and mutual goal-setting are necessary to ensure alignment. Talk about your individual and collective values and goals for your work and well-being to start. Think about the effects your work decisions will have on your overall happiness, lifestyle choices, and relationship dynamics. Be prepared to make choices that put your joy and contentment ahead of success or achievement as determined by outside standards. Have faith in your collaboration and place a high value on honest communication to overcome any obstacles or doubts that may surface.

**How can we resolve problems in our careers that result from different expectations or goals for a work-life balance? For example, one partner may favour career growth while the other may value spending more time with their family.**

Empathy, flexibility, and clear communication are necessary for conflict management. Start by honestly talking about each partner's expectations and preferences for work-life balance and how they fit with your family's objectives and the aims of your relationship. Work together to identify areas of agreement and consider possible concessions that would preserve a healthy balance while enabling both parties to feel supported in their goals in order to meet each other's needs and promote harmony in your relationship. Be prepared to modify your expectations and priorities as necessary.

**How can we handle scenarios where one partner's professional actions or choices affect the other partner's chances or goals, causing emotions of hatred or discontent?**

Managing effects calls for mutual assistance, communication, and empathy. Start by expressing and validating each other's emotions and worries over the potential impact of one partner's job decisions on the chances or goals of the other partner. Work together to develop a strategy that takes into account support, compromise, and joint goal setting in order to overcome any discrepancies or imbalances. Communicate your needs and concerns honestly, work as a team to find solutions, and take the initiative in resolving any sentiments of resentment or discontent.

# Chapter Four

*Overcoming the storm*

**How can we help one another through obstacles or career changes like burnout, job loss, or career stagnation?**

Empathy, encouragement, and helpful assistance are all part of supporting one another. Give each other's emotional support and validation for our experiences and feelings top priority when going through a difficult period. Provide helpful advice on how to find a job, create a CV, or take advantage of networking opportunities. Work together to develop a strategy for handling financial strains and negotiating ambiguities. Despite the difficulties, never forget to give priority to spending time together and engaging in activities that deepen your relationship.

**How can we make sure that our careers enhance one another and improve the dynamic of our partnership as a whole?**

Respect, gratitude, and cooperative goalsetting are all necessary to guarantee complementarity. Acknowledge and honour one another's accomplishments, talents, and achievements in your various fields of work. Seek out chances to encourage and assist one another in your career, whether it be through networking, mentoring, or common objectives. Openly discuss how your occupations affect the dynamics of your relationship and work to capitalize on each other's advantages to build a satisfying and encouraging alliance.

**In particular, how can we manage childcare, job progress, and domestic chores while living in a dual-career family?**
Managing two careers at the same time requires cooperation, open communication, and shared accountability. Talk openly about how to split up childcare and domestic chores so that each partner is treated fairly and equally. Look into childcare options or flexible work schedules that can satisfy the professional obligations of both couples. Make it a priority to check in frequently and make adjustments as necessary to make sure that both partners feel supported in their personal and professional lives.

**When career problems affect our relationship dynamic, how can we handle disagreements resulting from different work styles, priorities, or expectations?**

Empathy, flexibility, and clear communication are necessary for conflict management. Begin by accepting and validating one another's expectations, priorities, and working methods without passing judgment. Talk honestly about how these differences might affect the dynamic of your relationship, and work together to identify areas of agreement. Be prepared to give in and modify expectations as necessary to take into account the needs and preferences of one another. Concentrate on coming up with ideas that put mutual support and harmony first in your relationship and job.

**As a pair, how do we go through the decision-making process when it comes to significant career transitions like job changes, moves, or career pivots?**

Working together, communicating, and creating shared goals are essential when navigating a professional shift. Start by talking about your own goals and worries about the change and how it might affect your family and relationship. Work together to develop a strategy that takes into consideration the goals and desires of both parties and looks into possible avenues for development and support. Be prepared to review and modify your plan as necessary in light of changing conditions and mutual input.

**What should we do when one partner's job demands them to travel frequently or extensively, making it difficult for them and us to spend quality time together as a couple?**
Managing frequent travel requires preparation, prioritizing, and communicating. Start by being honest about how the trip has affected your relationship and how you both feel about it. When the travelling partner is at home, work together to plan a schedule that allows for quality time spent together, giving priority to activities that deepen your relationship. When you're away, use technology to stay in touch, make frequent video calls or send SMS, and plan for unique occasions or pleasant surprises to make the most of your time together.

**How do we handle circumstances where one partner's job necessitates them to move to a new nation or city, thereby upsetting our routines and social networks?**

Effective relocation requires open communication, flexibility, and teamwork. Start by talking about the relocation's possible advantages and disadvantages for each partner as well as how it fits with your long-term objectives as a marriage. Work together to develop a transition management strategy that takes into account housing, career opportunities, and support systems in the new area. As you consider the possibilities for professional and personal development that the move may present, keep each other's wants and worries in mind.

**In a relationship where one partner's work requires a disproportionate amount of time, effort, or emotional engagement, how can we still feel balanced and happy together?**

Setting limits, establishing priorities, and communicating openly are all necessary to maintain balance. Start by talking about how your relationship and personal wellness are affected by the imbalances in the demands of your profession. Work together to plan a timetable that emphasizes activities that deepen your relationship and leave time for quality time spent together. By being upfront about your wants and concerns and working as a team to find solutions, you may take the initiative to resolve any emotions of imbalance or resentment.

**What should we do when one partner's work demands frequent modification or retraining, creating uncertainty or shifting sources of income or stability?**

Managing uncertainty calls for adaptability, resilience, and teamwork. Start by recognizing and talking about the potential and difficulties related to one partner's professional obligations. Work together to develop a strategy for handling ambiguities and transitions that takes long-term objectives, emotional support, and financial stability into account. To meet each other's wants and goals and to keep your partnership feeling stable and secure, be prepared to modify your priorities and expectations as necessary.

**Instead of concentrating just on demands or expectations from the outside world, how can we make sure that our job trajectories reflect our beliefs and objectives as a couple?** Intentional decision-making, communication, and reflection are necessary to ensure alignment. Start by talking about your relationship's fundamental beliefs and priorities around your work and personal well-being. Think about how your job decisions affect your family objectives, overall happiness, and the dynamics of your relationships. Allow yourself to make choices that are consistent with your shared goals and beliefs, even if they deviate from demands or expectations from outside sources. Have faith in your collaboration and place a high value on honest communication to overcome any obstacles or doubts that may surface.

# Chapter Five

*Making sustainable decisions amidst odds*

**How do we approach scenarios in which one partner's work path may necessitate making concessions or sacrifices in other spheres of our lives, including postponing having children or following personal interests?**

Managing sacrifices calls for compromise, joint goal-setting, and empathy. Recognize and validate each other's sentiments and concerns over how one partner's job path may affect your relationship and personal goals. Talk honestly about how you can encourage one another's ambitions while still finding fulfilment and balance in other facets of your lives. To meet the needs and goals of both partners, be prepared to compromise and reorder priorities as necessary. Prioritize mutual support, harmony, and your partnership's growth while coming up with solutions, but don't forget to take the broader picture and long-term objectives into account.

**How do we handle circumstances in which we choose different career routes that result in disparities in pay, hours worked, or prospects for career advancement?**

Collaboration, empathy, and communication are necessary when navigating divergent career trajectories. Start by recognizing and talking about how your different professional paths may affect the dynamic of your relationship. Work together to develop a strategy that takes into consideration the needs and aims of both parties and look for ways to support and develop each other. Prioritize your relationship and common objectives while simultaneously being prepared to modify expectations and priorities as necessary to suit one another's career paths.

**How do we respond when outside influences, such as recessions or changes in the business, affect our hopes for a stable career as a couple?**

Resilience, adaptability, and mutual support are necessary for managing external stressors. Begin by recognizing and talking about the possible difficulties and unknowns related to outside influences on your career. Work together to develop a strategy for risk management that will minimize the effects on your relationship and overall well-being. Seek out tools and networks of support early on so that you can work as a team to overcome obstacles. Prioritize cultivating resilience and positivity within your partnership, and keep in mind that with shared resolve and support, you can overcome problems as a team.

**What should we do when one partner's profession demands significant compromises or sacrifices in other aspects of our lives, including postponing personal objectives or choosing a different career path?**

Managing sacrifices calls for compromise, joint goal-setting, and empathy. Begin by recognizing and talking about how one partner's professional demands affect your relationship and personal goals. Work together to develop a strategy that takes into consideration the requirements and objectives of both parties and look for ways to support and develop each other. To meet each other's needs and goals and to promote a sense of mutual support, harmony, and shared growth as a couple, be prepared to compromise and rearrange priorities as necessary.

## *About the Author*

**ADEGBOYE S. ADURAGBEMI** is a manager, business administrator, entrepreneur, and motivational speaker in Africa. ADEGBOYE has his BA from Yale University, IPMA from Adonai University, and a Master's in Business Administration (MBA) from the University of Salford, Manchester.

He was born in South Africa but is presently based in Nigeria as a motivational speaker and marriage counsellor in institutions, sectors, and seminars with young and upcoming managers all over Africa.

# Acknowledgements

I want to express my sincere gratitude to everyone who helped with the "FAQ on Communication in Marriage." Throughout this journey, their encouragement, insight, and support have been priceless.

I want to start by acknowledging the fact that, without God, this guide wouldn't have been possibly achieved.

And also to my spouse, who has always been motivating and supportive in making this task successful, I will always love and appreciate you.

I have many couples to appreciate who have shared their experiences, challenges, and victories with me over the years. Your openness, weakness, and tenacity have enhanced the book's pages and provided priceless insights into the difficulties of marriage communication.

My sincere gratitude goes out to my family and friends for their continuous support and encouragement during this journey. Your wise advice, tolerance, and words of support have helped me get through the complicated process of writing and releasing this book.

I sincerely thank the specialists and experts who have so kindly offered their knowledge and skills in marriage and communication. Your advice and thoughts have improved this book's quality and depth, and I really appreciate your contributions.

Finally, I would like to express my profound gratitude to all of the readers of this work. As you journey through the process of communication in your marriage, I hope that the knowledge, direction, and encouragement provided within these pages will be a source of inspiration and empowerment for you. I sincerely appreciate your help.